MW01009445

THE BIBLE, THE CHRISTIAN, AND
LATTER-DAY SAINTS

BY

GORDON R. LEWIS

PRESBYTERIAN AND REFORMED PUBLISHING CO.
Phillipsburg, New Jersey

THE AUTHOR

Dr. Gordon R. Lewis, Professor of Theology at Conservative Baptist Theological Seminary in Denver, Colorado, hails from Johnson City, New York. He began his theological education there at Baptist Bible Seminary, earned the A.B. in Theology at Gordon College (1948) and the graduate B.Th. at Faith Theological Seminary (1951). Adding an A.M. in philosophy from Syracuse University (1953), he did work at Cornell University and culminated his philosophical studies with a Ph.D. from Syracuse (1959).

Before coming to the Denver Seminary in 1958, Dr. Lewis pastored the People's Baptist Church, Hamilton Park, Delaware (1949-51), and taught seven years at Baptist Bible Seminary as Professor of Apologetics and Philosophy. While teaching he has held several interim pastorates in New York and Colorado. His wife graduated from Shelton College where she majored in Christian Education. The family includes two girls and a boy.

Published articles by Professor Lewis have appeared in *The Collegiate Challenge, Christianity Today,* and the *Bulletin of the Evangelical Theological Society.* For his Master's thesis, he critically examined Reinhold Niebuhr's influential view of dialectical truth, and for his dissertation Augustine's classical position on faith and reason.

Elected to the Theta Beta Phi Honorary Philosophical Society of Syracuse University, Dr. Lewis is also a member of the American Philosophical Association, The Metaphysical Society of America, The American Academy of Religion, and the Evangelical Theological Society.

PREFACE

Of little value are religious discussions which misrepresent positions, magnify incidentals, or manifest poor spirit. This study attempts to avoid all three pitfalls. A fair hearing is given to the group's primary sources. To eliminate unimportant issues attention has been focused upon the Bible's unique authority and the gospel's central claims. The intention has been to set forth the gospel to others in the same spirit the author would like to meet in those who differ with him.

Beliefs on which a person stakes his spiritual life for time and eternity necessarily concern him deeply. Because these issues are so important, it is hoped that each reader — whatever his emotional involvements — will carefully consider the scriptural conditions of eternal life.

Use of the term "cult" is not intended to disparage any person or association of persons. It is meant to point up a difference not covered by "denomination." Christian denominations, in spite of their intramural debates on other theological and ecclesiastical matters, give preeminence to the gospel of Christ. Cults, on the other hand, while claiming to be Christian alter or minimize the core of Christian faith — the gospel. This study goes forth with the prayer that all who claim to be followers of Christ may personally trust the Savior who was God, became flesh, died for our sins, and rose again, according to the Scriptures.

The author wishes to express his gratitude to the Reverend Edward L. Hayes, Associate Professor of Christian Education at Conservative Baptist Theological Seminary, for preparing the sections entitled "Teaching Suggestions."

The Biblical citations, unless otherwise indicated, are from the King James Version.

The Bible, The Christian, and
Latter-day Saints

Mormonism is America's fastest growing cult. Since 1900 Latter-day Saint membership has mushroomed from 250,000[1] to 1,952,328.[2] And most remarkably, during the last four years its missionary force has doubled! In 1959, 5,499 Mormon volunteers won some 7,019 converts; in 1962, 10,961 missionaries reaped 30,940 converts. As of March, 1963, there were 11,838 aggressive representatives who already had topped the total of converts for 1962, recording 39,894.[3]

What explains this unusual development? Most prominent of all the factors is the host of unsalaried young people who give a year or two of their lives for the cause. These fresh recruits every year impress millions of people. When their term of service is completed they return to various occupations with an unforgettable experience and a permanent ability to speak for their faith.

In the second place, every layman helps to spark the Mormon advance by unparalleled participation in the work.

> There is no paid or professional ministry. Thirty-two general officers and the presidents of missions are given living allowances. Add to this a few specialists and a staff of clerks who give their full working time to the church. These constitute all who may be classified as paid personnel. The great bulk of the work and responsibility is carried by the rank and file who receive no financial remuneration; who in fact, contribute generously not only of their time and talent, but of their means as well.[4]

A third factor contributing to Mormonism's success story is the efficient organization of its membership. Gordon B. Hinkley explains, "Everyone in the Church who is active and old enough to do something, generally has a responsibility. In fact, he may

5

have several. And usually the greatest enthusiasm for the cause is found among those who do the most."[5]

Fourth, each member is trained to perform his duties. "Education in all its implications, is . . . a concern of the Church. Accordingly, it has used its resources liberally in fostering schools. Moreover, it has constantly urged its youth to higher achievement and usefulness through education."[6] One study indicates that Utah leads the nation in the extent of adult education.[7] Four years after President Wilkinson took over the campus of Brigham Young University (1950) top Mormon leaders gathered to dedicate twenty-two modern buildings. Three years after that they returned to dedicate twelve more.[8] In 1958 "labor missionaries" completed a multimillion dollar Hawaiian college of twenty buildings on a 100-acre campus overlooking the Pacific.[9]

Mormonism spreads, for another thing, because its prosperity is appealing. Tithing, industry, and frugality have produced a powerful religious empire.

> Unique among religions, the Mormon church efficiently runs a sugar company, grain mills and elevators, a department store, banks, newspapers, a radio and television station, a hotel and luxurious new hotel-motel, ranches, feed lots and farms to name just a few enterprises. . . . It raises peanuts in Texas, grapefruit in Arizona, prizewinning dairy stock in New Jersey and beef cattle in Florida, Georgia and Canada.[10]

As a result, no Mormon need fear extreme poverty. Built into his religion is a social security program.

> Mormonism is a self-reliant society which distributes the bounty of all its people to any member in need. Mormons do not believe in government doles. There is freedom from want in a chain of farms, storehouses, and granaries that keep on hand — together with what is stored by each family — enough food and clothing to supply *every* Mormon for a full year.[11]

Mormon prosperity is demonstrated also in extensive construction. A 38-story denominational building is going up in Salt Lake City and another skyscraper is rising on Manhattan's Fifth Avenue. Churches are going up so rapidly that on the average Latter-day Saints dedicate a building a day.[12]

In the last place the amazing growth of Mormonism must be attributed in some measure to its attractive teaching. Alleging a continuing revelation and priesthood, the Latter-day Saints appeal to many who want visible sources of divine authority. Eschewing the complicated doctrines of the Trinity and imputed righteousness, they exalt the simple and "reasonable" and join those who repudiate the notoriously offensive doctrines of predestination and eternal punishment. They emphasize, as does the *Book of Mormon*, "Men are that they might have joy" (II Nephi 2:25).

It is the doctrine of the Church of Jesus Christ of Latter-day Saints which primarily concerns evangelical Christians. Knowing that one's eternal life depends upon his acceptance of the gospel message, Christians ask whether Mormons believe that truth. With all their joys of prosperity and success, have they found the highest satisfaction of all — the joy of those "whose transgression is forgiven, whose sin is covered" (Ps. 32:1)? In order to help any who may not share the saving grace of God, we ask the following seven questions. May it please the Holy Spirit to grant many who have not enjoyed it, the "full assurance" of divine pardon (Col. 2:2).

1. *Authority*

In any discussion of religion, if the parties involved accept different sources of authoritative teaching, agreement will be unlikely. To determine whether this may be the case with a Mormon friend, ask this pointed question: "Do you base your beliefs on revelations or sacred writings other than the Bible?"

Mormons acknowledge the divine authority, not only of the Bible, but also of the *Book of Mormon, The Doctrine and Covenants, The Pearl of Great Price*, and continuous revelation in the official teaching of the President of the church. Following founder Joseph Smith's "Articles of Faith (8,9) they say, "We believe the Bible to be the word of God as far as it is translated correctly; we also believe the *Book of Mormon* to be the word of God. We believe all that God has revealed, and all that He does now reveal and we believe that He will yet reveal many great and important things pertaining to the Kingdom of God." Where do Mormons look for these future revelations?

So long as the Lord has any communication to make to the children of men, or any instructions to impart to His Church, He will make such communication through the legally appointed channel of the Priesthood; He will never go outside of it, as long, at least, as the Church of Jesus Christ of Latter-day Saints exists in its present form on the earth.[13]

Because of their doctrine of continuous revelation Latter-day Saints have strong words for Christians who insist that the Bible is the sufficient and only infallible rule of faith and practice. Smith, in the *Book of Mormon*, calls such Christians "Gentiles" and fools,"

Many of the Gentiles shall say: A Bible! A Bible! We have got a Bible, and there cannot be any more Bible, But thus saith the Lord God: . . . Thou fool, that shall say: A Bible, we have got a Bible, and we need no more Bible . . . Wherefore murmur ye, because that ye shall receive more of my word? . . . Because that ye have a Bible ye need not suppose that it contains all my words; neither need ye suppose that I have not caused more to be written" (II Nephi 29:3-10).

Are people unchristian and foolish for questioning the supposed divine authority of Mormon revelations? To the contrary, there are good reasons for concluding Mormons have been misled in adding other books to the Biblical revelation.

For one thing, Mormons are not alone in claiming continued revelation. Christian Scientists add Mary Baker Eddy's *Science and Health with Key to the Scriptures* to the Bible; the Muslims have their *Koran*; and Spiritualists think their repeated seances produce messages from the other world. No one can be expected to accept all these purported revelations without consideration. And why should we be favorably disposed toward Latter-day Saint revelations? Because the Church has grown rapidly? So did Islam and Christian Science. Are all other churches apostate and Mormons alone the source of divine ministry in these latter days? But according to Jehovah's Witnesses Mormons as well as others are part of the great apostasy and Witnesses alone constitute God's organization. In view of such contradictory and pretentious claims, Mormons will pardon us if we examine their alleged revelations more closely.

The issue is not whether the sacred writings of the Church of Jesus Christ of Latter-day Saints are popular or unpopular, but whether they are true or false. How then can we test the truth of an alleged revelation? We may ask: (1) if it is self-consistent, and (2) if it is in accord with available evidence. A mother checks the consistency of her child's story and then compares it with what she knows of the facts of the case. A judge hearing the explanation of a suspect examines it for its consistency in itself and its correlation with all the relevant evidence. Similarly, a person confronted by an alleged revelation tests its consistency and its conformity with all significant data. What God says is never contraidictory; He cannot deny Himself (II Tim. 2:13). It is utterly impossible for God to lie (Tit. 1:2; Heb. 6:18; Num. 23:19). Therefore God's truth will not misrepresent historical truth. Mormons who risk so much on the validity of their alleged revelations should not fear this twofold test. First, are the Latter-day Saint scriptures logically consistent?

Difficult indeed is the task of one who tries to harmonize the teaching of Mormon revelations on any given subject. Polygamy, for example, is both commanded and condemned. According to one attempt to interpret this matter with some consistency the Mormons say polygamy as a lustful practice is condemned, but in their religion it is not lustful because many Mormon men had died and it was necessary to repopulate "Zion." But it was on July 12, 1843, in Nauvoo, Illinois, that Joseph Smith received the "revelation" concerning polygamy. The arduous journey to Utah had not yet taken its toll! Others will suggest that the contradiction is harmonized if we realize the "eternal covenant" with its attendant polygamy still stands. President Wilford Woodruff in 1890 under pressure of the United States Government, received a "revelation" to discontinue not the eternal covenant but the practice of polygamy. However, the covenant makes the practice eternal when it says, "If ye abide not in that covenant then are ye damned" (*Doctrines and Covenants* 132). It is difficult to see how even a later revelation could change such an emphatic eternal covenant.

But no alleged revelation can correct the contradiction in the polygamy passages regarding the wives of David and Solomon. The *Book of Mormon* decries "wicked practices, such as like unto David of old desiring many wives and concubines, and also Solomon, his son" (Jacob 1:15). Again, "Behold David and Solomon truly had many wives and concubines, which thing was abominable before me, saith the Lord" (Jacob 2:24). Contrast the latter "revelation"

9

seeking to support polygamy by reference to the cases of David and Solomon. "David also received many wives and concubines, and also Solomon, . . . and David's wives and concubines were given unto him of me, by the hand of Nathan . . . and in none of these things did he sin against me save in the case of Uriah and his wife" (*Doctrines and Covenants* 132). Can a conscientious Mormon believe the plurality of David and Solomon's wives both a gift of God without sin as the *Doctrines and Covenants* teaches and a wicked and abominable practice in the sight of God as the *Book of Mormon* teaches. If a Mormon practices polygamy he will be condemned by one of his sacred writings; if he does not practice polygamy he will "be damned" by the other.

Mormon revelations are equally contradictory with respect to the question of whether there is one God or many. The *Book of Mormon* knows nothing of many Gods, but teaches the unity of Father, Son, and Holy Spirit in typical Trinitarian terminology. Smith wrote, "they are one God" (Mosiah 15:4). He refers to "Christ the Son, and God the Father, and the Holy Spirit, which is one Eternal God" (Alma 11:44). The redeemed, the *Book of Mormon* says, will sing praises around the throne "unto the Father, and unto the Son, and unto the Holy Ghost, which are one God" (Mormon 7:7). And on Smith's word this is "the only and true doctrine of the Father, and of the Son, and of the Holy Ghost, which is one God, without end" (II Nephi 31:21). When Zeezrom talked with Amulek, a man who said nothing contrary to the Spirit of the Lord, Zeezrom asked, "Is there more than one God?" Amulek answered, "No" (Alma 11:28-9).

In marked contrast to all this evidence of the oneness of the Godhead in the *Book of Mormon*, is the teaching of other Mormon revelations. Apparently Smith's ideas changed, not only on polygamy, but also on theology. He writes of "a time to come in the which, nothing shall be withheld, whether there be one God or many gods, *they* shall be manifest" (*D & C* 121:32). When it came time to create the world, the Gods had an argument.

> The Lord said, who shall I send? And one answered like unto the Son of Man, Here am I, send me. And another answered and said, Here am I, send me. And the Lord said, I will send the first. And the second was angry, and kept not his first estate, and at that day, many followed after him (*Pearl of Great Price*, Abraham, p. 41).

There follows the creation story with the name for God changed to Gods. The Gods said, ordered, organized, prepared, etc., "And the Gods said among themselves, On the seventh time we will end our work which we have counseled; and we will rest on the seventh time from all our work. . . . And thus were their decisions at the time that they counseled among themselves to form the heavens and the earth" (Abraham, p. 44). Shall a Mormon accept these later "revelations" of many Gods or the only true doctrine of the one God in the *Book of Mormon?* Latter-day Saints may try to explain the unity of Gods as one of thought and purpose, but that can hardly have been the intent of Joseph Smith's earlier statements. The inconsistency of their sacred writings remains.

The Mormons, if they believe their scriptures, must believe that all things were created and some things were not created! "The elements are eternal," according to *Doctrines and Covenants* (93: 33). Consequently Talmadge argues, God "certainly did not create, in the sense of bringing into primal existence, the ultimate elements of the materials of which the earth consists."[14] On the other hand, the *Book of Mormon* teaches "he hath created all things, both the heavens and the earth, and all things that in them are, both things to act and things to be acted upon" (II Nephi 2:14). If a more emphatic statement is needed, Smith also says, "Yea, he is the very Eternal Father of heaven and of earth, and all things which in them are; he is the beginning and the end, the first and the last" (Alma 11:39). Now if all things, whether active or passive, owe their existence to God, not even the physical elements missed being created. How can a Mormon believe that the elements are both eternal and created?

The Mormon scriptures also contradict the Bible. God the Father, according to *Doctrines and Covenants*, has "a body of flesh and bones as tangible as man's (130:22b). But John 4:24 teaches, "God is spirit," and Jesus said, ". . . a spirit hath not flesh and bones as ye see me have" (Lk. 24:39). The Mormon scriptures teach that God is visible; the Bible teaches God is invisible (I Tim. 1:17; 6:16). Can a Mormon believe that God is a visible body and that God is an invisible Spirit?

A last instance of contradiction occurs in connection with the birthplace of Christ. Although the Bible reports Christ's birth in Bethlehem (Micah 5:2; Mt. 2:1,5), the *Book of Mormon* "predicts"

Jesus will be born in Jerusalem (Alma 7:9,10). Mormons attempt to explain this discrepancy by alleging that Jerusalem was once a state which included Bethlehem. But evidence for this is non-existent. They are two distinct cities five miles apart. Christ could not possibly have been born in both. One or the other of these accounts is not true. A Latter-day Saint cannot logically accept both.

Talmadge claims Mormon writings are free from contradiction, admitting the validity of this test.[15] But his claim does not stand examination. No one can believe at the same time that polygamy is eternally approved and not proper now, that there is but one God and there are many Gods, that God the Father is flesh and bones and invisible spirit, that God did not create the elements of nature but created everything there is, and that Jesus was born in both Jerusalem and Bethlehem. Even on a theory of continuous revelation God cannot deny Himself. Both Christians and Mormons agree that the Bible originates with God. But who can believe writings which contradict themselves and the Bible come from God?

Mormon claims, if true, would necessarily accord with the relevant facts as well as the law of contradiction. The Book of Mormon provides abundant opportunity for factual examination. It purports to present the history of two great civilizations in South and North America from about 600 B.C. to A.D. 421. At the command of God two Jewish brothers, Nephi and Laman, sailed with their families from Jerusalem in a home-made boat and landed in South America around 590 B.C. In spite of continued "revelations" from God the descendants warred with each other as they travelled northward. The dark skinned Lamanites who survived gave birth to many of the American Indians. Before the Nephites were wiped out one of their leaders by the name of Mormon buried plates inscribed with the history of these peoples in "reformed Egyptian hieroglyphics." The records remained in the hill Cumorah near Palmyra, New York, until Joseph Smith "dug them up" and "translated" them in 1830.

Is this story true? Several difficulties with it are noted by the impartial government sponsored Smithsonian Institution's Bureau of American Ethnology in Washington, D. C. Since Mormon missionaries often allege support from this source, inquiries are frequent. A mimeographed "Statement Regarding the Book of Mormon" says

"Smithsonian archeologists see no connection between the archeology of the New World and the subject matter of the Book (of Mormon)." The same "statement" adds the specific points which follow.

Although anthropologically a race stemming from Jews in Palestine would have the characteristics of Mediterranean Caucasoid, "The physical type of the American Indian is basically Mongoloid."

Instead of travelling by boat, about 600 B.C., "It is believed that the ancestors of the present Indians came into the New World — probably over a land bridge known to have existed in the Bering Strait region during the last Ice Age — in a continuing series of migrations beginning about 30,000 years ago."

Rather than bringing a culture from the old world, "Extensive archaeological researches in southern Mexico and Central America clearly indicate that the civilizations of these regions developed locally from simple beginnings without the aid of outside stimulus."

Were the first Easterners to reach America Jews? "Present evidence indicates that the first people to reach America from the East were Norsemen who arrived in the northeastern part of North America around 1000 A.D."

And what about a language called "reformed Egyptian hieroglyphics"? We know of no authentic cases of ancient Egyptian or Hebrew writing having been found in the New World. Reports of findings of Egyptian influence in the Mexican and Central American area have been published in newspapers and magazines from time to time, but thus far no reputable Egyptologist has been able to discover any relationship between remains and those in Egypt."[16]

In view of these conclusions the Smithsonian Institution can hardly be alleged by overly enthusiastic young missionaries to have employed the Book of Mormon in its scientific research. Scientific knowledge may still be very limited, it is true. We do not know what may be discovered in future investigations. But present knowledge indicates that the Mormon story is false in every detail.

In arguing for the validity of the "reformed Egyptian" language Mormons will adduce the testimony of two linguists in New York City about 1830. The only two contemporaries qualified to identify the language are featured in the *Pearl of Great Price* and an excerpt from it published in the popular pamphlet, "Joseph Smith Tells His Own Story."[17] According to these sources, Martin Harris, a friend of Smith's, took a copy of some of the plates and their translation to Dr. Mitchell and Professor Anthon in New York City. Columbia University's professor Anthon said the translated plates were Egyptian correctly translated, and gave Harris a certificate to that effect, but when he heard how the plates were discovered tore up the certificate. Harris then left and "went to Dr. Mitchell, who sanctioned what Professor Anthon had said respecting both the characters and the translation."[18]

This account is exploded by none other than Professor Anthon himself. In a letter addressed to Mr. E. D. Howe, Painesville, Ohio, February 17, 1834, Anthon wrote with italicized emphasis, "The whole story about my having pronounced the Mormonite inscription to be 'reformed Egyptian hieroglyphics' *is perfectly false.*" He stated that a simple farmer had called on him with a note from Dr. Mitchell "requesting me to decipher, if possible, a paper which . . . Dr. Mitchell confessed he had been unable to understand." Thus Dr. Mitchell's alleged testimony is negated. Anthon further emphasized:

This paper was in fact a singular scrawl. It consisted of crooked characters disposed in columns and had evidently been prepared by some person who had before him at the time a book containing various alphabets. Greek and Hebrew letters, crosses, and flourishes, Roman letters inverted or placed sideways, were arranged in perpendicular columns, and the whole ended in a rude delineation of a circle, divided into various compartments, decked with strange marks, and evidently copied after the Mexican Calendar given by Humboldt, but copied in such a way as not to betray the source whence it was derived. . . . the paper contained anything else but "Egyptian hieroglyphics."[19]

Other aspects of Smith's tale do not square with facts. The manner in which he "translated" these most unusual characters is incredible. David Whitmer, at whose home much of the work was done, included an explanation in his sermon, "An Address to All Believers in Christ."

I will now give you a description of the manner in which the Book of Mormon was translated. Joseph Smith would put the seer stone into a hat, and put his face in the hat, drawing it closely around his face to exclude the light; and in the darkness the spiritual light would shine. A piece of something resembling parchment would appear, and on that appeared writing. One character at a time would appear, and under it was the interpretation in English. Brother Joseph would read off the English to Oliver Cowdery, who was his principal scribe, and when it was written down and repeated to Brother Joseph to see if it was correct, then it would disappear and another character with the interpretation would appear. Thus the Book of Mormon was translated by the gift and power of God, and not by any power of man.[20]

As a result of this allegedly supernatural activity Smith said, "I told the brethren that the Book of Mormon was the most correct of any book on earth, and the keystone of our religion, and a man would get nearer to God by abiding by its precepts than by any other book."[21] Strange that this "most correct" book in later editions suffered extensive alteration by men not supernaturally endowed. In the first 25 pages there were more than 500 changes,[22] and in the whole book more than 2,800 not counting punctuation.[23]

If Smith's work was done independently from the plates as claimed, it is impossible to account for extensive sections lifted right out of the King James translation. The golden plates were, according to no less an authority than Joseph Smith, buried from A.D. 420 until he dug them up. The alleged writers of the plates could have had no contact with a translation of the Bible made in A.D. 1611. Nevertheless the Book of Mormon plagiarizes at least twenty-seven thousand words from the King James translation.[24] And some of these represent readings in all probability not in the inspired original (I Jn. 5:7; III Nephi 11:27,36) and not the best rendering of what does stand in the original.[25] Furthermore some of the "predictions" of Christ's first coming supposed to be given hundreds of years in advance show obvious dependence upon King James expressions.

In spite of all this, Mormons will produce the testimony of eleven witnesses who saw the plates Smith is said to have translated. They are presented in two groups. The three witnesses, Oliver Cowdery, David Whitmer, and Martin Harris, signed a statement to the effect that they saw the engraved plates. An angel came down from heaven and laid them before their eyes and God's voice declared that the work was true. Eight witnesses are also highly publicized, largely Whitmers and Smiths: "Christian Whitmer, Jacob Whitmer, Peter Whitmer, Jr., John Whitmer, Hiram Page, Joseph Smith, Sen., Hyrum Smith, and Samuel Smith. These say Joseph Smith showed them plates having the appearance of gold and curious engravings. "For we have seen and hefted, and know of a surety, that the said Smith has got the plates of which we have spoken."[26]

How valuable is all this testimony? Not one of these people was qualified to recognize another language. If they literally saw plates with "curious" markings and "hefted" them, this is of no scholarly significance. And in what way did they "see" them? Prior to their view of the plates, Smith gave the three witnesses this "revelation":

> Behold, I say unto you, that you must rely upon my word, which if you do with full purpose of heart, you shall have a view of the plates, and also of the breastplate, the sword of Laban, the Urim and Thummin. . . . And it is by your faith that you shall obtain a view of them . . . And ye shall testify that you have seen them even as my servant Joseph Smith, Jun., has seen them; for it is by my power that he has seen them, and it is because he had faith. (*Doctrines and Covenants* 17:1,2,5).

A prominent citizen of Palmyra asked Martin Harris, "Did you see the plates with your natural eyes, just as you see this pencil case in my hand? Now say yes or no." Harris answered, "Why, I did not see them as I do that pencil case, I saw them with the eye of faith. I saw them just as distinctly as I see anything around me — though at the time they were covered over with a cloth."[27] David Whitmer explained, "Suppose that you had a friend whose character was such that you knew it impossible that he could lie; then, if he described a city to you which you had never seen, could you not, by the eye of faith see the city just as he described it?"[28] Here is admission from one who should know, that we have not eleven literal witnesses, but just one, Joseph Smith. If people are looking for confirmation of Smith's story, they do not have it in the testimony of such "witnesses." They apparently took Smith's word for the very existence of plates. But he too saw them by faith as the passage from *Doctrines and Covenants* (17:5) declares. In all probability, then, there actually were no literally visible gold plates at all! And when the faith of these witnesses waned, eight of the eleven defected from the Church of Jesus Christ of Latter-day Saints.[29]

Where then did Smith obtain his ideas? One major source was the Bible. Not only did he quote whole chapters and sections, but he also seems to have imitated many of its stories. A second source may have been Solomon Spaulding's historical novel, *The Manuscript Found*. Mormons often disparage any idea of dependence on another book, *The Manuscript Story*. In so doing they fail to answer such students of Mormonism as E. D. Howe, Pomeroy Tucker, William A. Linn, James D. Bales, and Walter R. Martin. One such scholar, J. H. Beadle concludes, "The true theory no doubt is, that the writing of Spaulding (*The Manuscript Found*) was taken by Smith, Rigdon, Cowdery and others, as the suggestion and idea of their work; but it was greatly modified and interpolated by them."[30] A third source is a distant relative of Joseph Smith's father, Rev. Ethan Smith, who visited the family in 1822 and again in 1825. The Congregational minister thought the American Indians were descendants of the lost tribes of Israel, and sought the help of Joseph in finding Indian relics in the hill Cumorah. Joseph had access to his *View of the Hebrews*.[31] Also in circulation were James Adair's *History of the American Indians*, published in 1775, and Abbe Clavigero's *History of Mexico*, printed in 1787.[32] Add to these materials the apt imagination of Joseph Smith, a "peek stone adict" known for hunting buried treasure,[33] and the elements of the *Book of Mormon* seem adequately explained without any revelations.

The story of its supernatural origin fails to fit the facts; instead, the facts confirm the book's fallibility. It contains many anachronisms and blunders. Laban wielded a sword made of "the most precious steel" before 592 B.C.[34] (I Nephi 4:9). Although compasses are thought to have originated around A.D. 1000,[34] Nephi sailed across the ocean with the aid of a compass around 600 B.C. (I Nephi 18:12). The earliest French developed from Latin about A.D. 700,[35] but Jacob, before A.D. 421 concludes his book, by bidding his brethren "adieu" (Jacob 7:27, dated 544 B.C. and A.D. 421). Walter R. Martin concludes that the *Book of Mormon* "betrays a great lack of information and background on the subject of world history and the history of the Jewish people."[36]

But what about the prophecies of the *Book of Mormon* and the *Doctrines and Covenants*? Latter-day Saints often claim that these prove the supernatural origin of the book. And some of Smith's prophecies have come to pass. In 1844 he predicted Christ would not return to earth in the next forty years. Smith said his own name would be held for good and evil among all nations. Such prophecies, however, are not of sufficient detail and significance of themselves to prove supernatural knowledge. Others were based upon discernible trends, such as that of the Civil War, predicted December 25, 1832 (*Doctrines and Covenants* 87). At the time

Smith made the prophecy the nation expected war. On July 14, 1832, Congress passed a tariff act which South Carolina, threatening to secede, declared null and void. President Jackson sent the nation's troops and warships to Charleston. Governor Hayne vowed to defend his state's sovereignty or die "beneath its ruins."[37] Joseph Smith was not alone in predicting civil war at that dark Christmas season. Are all who did recipients of "revelation"? Furthermore, included in Smith's prediction was the assertion, ". . . then war shall be poured out upon all nations." This does not fit the facts; the Civil War did not develop into a world war.

Fifty-eight prophecies of Joseph Smith examined in detail by G. T. Harrison failed to come to pass. The former third generation Mormon concludes:

> A baseball player who did not have a higher rating as a ball player than Joseph Smith's average as a true prophet, could not even play on the cinderlot team. He would not even be able to catch a ball. After studied calculation we find his rating as a prophet to be: No hits. No runs. 58 errors.[38]

Now, even Mormon scientists acknowledge that the *Book of Mormon* story has yet to be shown to fit the facts. When Mormon missionaries say that more things have been proven true by archeology in the *Book of Mormon* than in the Bible, they may be refuted by professors of Brigham Young University, Provo, Utah. Members of the University Archeological Society writing in the Society's *Newsletter* are emphatic. "The statement that the Book of Mormon has already been proved by archeology is misleading. . . . That such an idea could exist indicates the ignorance of our people with regard to what is going on in the historical and anthropological sciences."[39] Joseph E. Vincent admits:

> Many times, Mormon missionaries have told their investigators that such late-period ruins as Monte Alban (periods III-V), Yagul, and Mitla were built by the Nephites and that the archeologists would confirm this. Both claims are untrue. However, the earliest periods of the area, Monte Alban I and II, although as yet little known, are of Preclassic (i.e., Book of Mormon period) date. One may think of these earlier peoples as Jaredites or Nephites, but if so it must be on the basis of faith, not archeology, for so far there is no explicit evidence that the Book of Mormon peoples occupied this area (Oaxaca, in the Isthmus of Tehuantepec area of Mexico).[40]

In addition these scholars acknowledge that not one city mentioned in the *Book of Mormon* has been identified, and that Mormon missionaries have made unsupportable claims to the effect that non-Mormon archeologists have used the book in their research.[41]

It seems well within the bounds of evidence to conclude, then, that the Latter-day Saint scriptures are not only inconsistent, but unsupported by known facts. There is no evidence of the alleged races, ocean voyage, arrival in the new world, transplantation of culture, engraved plates, reformed Egyptian hieroglyphics, or any possibility to translate a foreign language on the part of the "translator." Evidence does show adequate sources of the material, and its human and erroneous character in spite of numerous corrections since the first edition.

Any mother finding her child involved in such contradictions and falsehoods as these would conclude he did not speak the truth. A judge who caught a suspect in several inconsistencies and fabrications would doubt that he told the whole truth and nothing but the truth. It is difficult to see how any other conclusion is justified with respect to the sacred writings of Mormonism.

Latter-day Saints may still insist that Joseph Smith claimed to be a prophet. Suppose we grant the possibility of prophets in the twentieth century. How would we distinguish a true prophet from a false one? We would follow the counsel given the ancient Israelites who cried out, "How shall we know the word which the Lord hath not spoken?" (Deut. 18:21). Two tests were given; the first is doctrinal. Any alleged prophet's teaching about God must be consistent with revelation to that point. Even though the self-acclaimed prophet is able to perform signs and wonders, if he says, "Let us go after other gods which thou hast not known, and let us serve them; thou shalt not hearken unto the words of that prophet, or that dreamer of dreams" (Deut. 13:2-3). Whoever directs people to another god, however wonderful his works, is not a true prophet of God. Joseph Smith's flesh-and-bones god is not the God of the Bible or Christianity. Can he be a true prophet?

The second test of a true prophet requires that every predictive sign must come to pass. Suppose a self-appointed prophet teaches the truth concerning God. Is that a sufficient guarantee of his authenticity? The Scriptures say, "When a prophet speaketh in the name of the Lord, if the thing follow not nor come to pass, that is the thing which the Lord hath not spoken, but the prophet hath spoken it presumptuously: thou shalt not be afraid of him" (Deut. 18:21-22). Whoever predicts things which fail to take place is not a true prophet of God. Joseph Smith's predictions, in numerous cases, failed to come to pass. Can he be a true prophet? May God use this evidence to deliver many sincere people from enslavement to counterfeit "revelation." Mormons who refuse to follow this evidence where it leads, nevertheless, affirm belief in the Bible, and on that basis the remaining questions can be discussed.

2. *The Gospel*

A Christian may well ask a Latter-day Saint, "Is your main business the preaching of the gospel?" Mormons may well answer, "Indeed, it is. Our Church is built upon the gospel." Others remain in an "awful state of blindness" because "the plain and most precious parts of the gospel of the Lamb . . . have been kept back by that abominable church" (I Nephi 13:32). It is precisely to restore the gospel lost in an apostate church that the Church of Jesus Christ of Latter-day Saints has been raised up. It fulfills the prediction, "I will bring forth unto them, in mine own power, much of my gospel, which shall be plain and precious, saith the Lamb" (I Nephi 13:34). Churches remain Christ's church, the Lord is quoted as saying, only "if it so be that they are built upon my gospel" (3 Nephi 27:8).

Is the present Church of Jesus Christ of Latter-day Saints now giving pre-eminence to the gospel? Because of the complexity of the program, that commendable original intention may not in fact be achieved. One or more of Mormonism's other facets which arise from varied sources may usurp the primary place of the gospel. From Roman Catholicism comes the emphasis upon a hierarchy headed not by a pope but a president who expresses present day revelations from God to man. The Campbellites suggested the concept of baptismal regeneration which leads to fascination with baptism for the dead. Judaism is reflected in a prominent priesthood and preoccupation with legalistic works. Smith's and Young's experiences in Masonry provided ideas of secret symbolism and temple ceremonies. The notion of polygamy and blood atonement (by men

20

now), as well as of a modern prophet, come from Islam. Mohammed so impressed Joseph Smith that he designated himself "the modern Mohammed." And the Rosicrucian doctrine that men are gods in embryo sparked Smith's theory that "As man is, God once was, as God is, man may become."[42]

Among these multiple interests the gospel may easily take second place. That may have happened in an article by LeRoy E. Cowles entitled, "Church of Jesus Christ of Latter-day Saints." After only one sentence about Christ's atonement, the former president of the University of Utah discusses Mormon history, organization, administration, education, temples, missions, giving, and welfare.[43] On the other hand, apostle Richard Evans, in "What is a Mormon?" emphasizes that Joseph Smith "was commissioned of God to effect a 'restoration' of the Gospel of Jesus Christ and to open a new Gospel 'dispensation'." Although the gospel of Jesus Christ was proclaimed in the heavens before the world was, Evans explains, a last restoration occurred in the early nineteenth century beginning "the dispensation of the fullness of times."[44] In theory, if not always in practice, Mormonism intends to give pre-eminence to the restored gospel.

Christians have a question, however, Is the Mormon message in fact the Biblical gospel? The popular pictorial book, *The Mormon Story*, claims it is.

> The old but newly revealed Gospel of Jesus Christ that Joseph Smith was to share with his fellow men was the same as had been given to the "Jews" and "Gentiles" in Palestine and also to the ancient inhabitants (Nephites) in the Americas nearly 2000 years ago by Jesus Christ himself in person.[45]

Can Mormons make good this claim? They must or be discredited! Their own Biblical authority insists "though we (apostles) or an angel from heaven (Moroni) preach any other gospel unto you than that which we have preached to you, let him be accursed" (Gal. 1:8). For the sake of their own souls Mormons must honestly face this destiny-determining issue. Have they believed the one true gospel? The remaining questions of this study will serve to formulate an answer to this fundamental consideration.

3. *Christ*

At the heart of the Biblical gospel is the doctrine of the deity and incarnation of Jesus Christ. Suppose you ask a Mormon if he believes these truths. Make your question specific: "Do you believe that Jesus is the Christ (the anointed Messiah) who was God (Jn. 1:1) and became flesh (Jn. 1:14)?" What reply is a Mormon likely to give?

One of the most influential Mormon authors, James E. Talmadge, answers emphatically:

> No one professing a belief in Christianity can consistently accept the Holy Scriptures as genuine and deny the preexistence of Christ, or doubt that before the birth of the Holy One as Mary's babe in Bethlehem of Judea, He had lived with the Father as an unembodied spirit, the Firstborn of the Father's children. . . . Christ while a man among men repeatedly affirmed the fact of His antemortal life that he came forth from the Father, and would return to the Father on the completion of His mission in mortality.[46]

But however emphatically Christ's pre-existence is asserted, Mormons do not teach His deity in a Trinitarian sense. Christ is not the Son of God as orthodox Christians have understood the Scripture, but a "spirit-child of God" as all human beings are supposed to have been prior to their birth. Mormon terminology is clarified by Lowell L. Bennion's chart of "Stages and Opportunities in Man's Eternal Life."[47]

When God, "the most intelligent" of the eternal intelligences, decided to clothe the others with spiritual form, Christ was the first-begotten. Christ was not eternally the Father's Son; He was not eternally pre-eminent. He "was the Firstborn Spirit Child, and from that day forward he has had, in all things, the pre-eminence."[48] Clearly then, Mormons do not teach that Christ was essentially one with the Father, or that He was God. And they are willing to alter Scripture which teaches Christ's actual deity. Their treatment of John 1:1 is similar to that of Jehovah's Witnesses. Senator Wallace F. Bennett in his book, *Why I Am A Mormon*, with the doctrinal "imprimatur" of the President of the L.D.S. Washington Stake, says, "We would read it thus: In the beginning was Jesus, and Jesus was with God, and Jesus was |a| God."[49] Jehovah's Witnesses, believing in only one God, print "a god" with a small letter "g"; Mormons believing in many Gods, translate it with a capital "G." But by inserting "a" before "God" both deny the true deity of Jesus Christ who is eternally and essentially one with the Father and the Spirit. John 1:1 still stands! "The Word was God."

Unable to understand and accept the actual deity of Jesus Christ or the doctrine of the Trinity, the Mormons nevertheless believe Jesus was the Messiah.

> We hold that Jesus Christ was the one and only Being fitted to become the Savior and Redeemer of the world, for the following reasons: (1) He is the only sinless Man who has ever walked the earth. (2) He is the Only Begotten of the Eternal Father in the flesh, and therefore the only Being born to earth possessing in their fulness the attributes and power of both Godhood and manhood. (3) He is the One who had been chosen in the primeval council of the Gods and foreordained to this service.[50]

But all such praise of Christ as redeemer falls far short of Christian teaching. If Jesus was not the one true God, He is unable to save. And what is this "council of the Gods"? They are three separately and physically distinct Gods, according to Apostle Talmadge. He explains:

> Three personages composing the great presiding council of the universe have revealed themselves to man: (1) God the eternal Father; (2) His Son, Jesus Christ; and (3) the Holy Ghost. That these three are held to be separate individuals, physically distinct from each other is demonstrated by the accepted records of divine dealings with man.[51]

Then in flatly repudiating the doctrine of the Trinity, Talmadge adds, "This cannot rationally be construed to mean that the Father, the Son, and the Holy Ghost are one in substance."[52]

Why is the unity of the Godhead irrational to Talmadge? Two, let alone three, material things cannot occupy the same space at the same time! And, "Admitting the personality of God, we are compelled to accept the fact of His materiality."[53] Why so? Then it becomes impossible to understand the personality of "intelligences," "spirit-children," "unembodied spirits," and the Holy Spirit! Nevertheless they teach that the Father and Son, if not the Holy Spirit, have literal flesh-and-bones bodies.

23

> We know that both the Father and the Son are in form and stature
> perfect men; each of them possesses a tangible body, infinitely pure
> and perfect and attended by transcendent glory, nevertheless a body
> of flesh and bones.[54]

If, as Talmadge argues, personality requires a flesh-and-bones body, the Holy Spirit must not be a person. But that contradicts what Joseph Smith wrote by alleged revelation, when he said, ". . . the Holy Ghost has not a body of flesh and bones, but is a personage of spirit" (*Doctrines and Covenants* 130:22). The Christian doctrine of the Trinity simply says that from all eternity all three members of the Godhead were personages of the spirit. As such they have no flesh-and-bones body. They are not therefore bound by the physical law that two things cannot dwell in the same place at the same time. As infinite spirits they are unlimited by space and time. In order that Mormons may see that God is one, and that Jesus Christ is God, they must be helped to understand that personality does not require a physical organism.

Christians can help Latter-day Saints by emphasizing that God is spirit (Jn. 4:24), and that our risen Lord taught, "a spirit hath not flesh and bones" Lk. 24:39). That is why the Bible says that God is invisible (I Tim. 1:17; 6:16; Heb. 11:27), and that "No man hath seen God at any time" (Jn. 1:18; 5:37). And that is why Joseph Smith is mistaken when He claims to have seen the Father as well as the incarnate Son. Although there is no literal physical vision of God, there is another way of "seeing him who is invisible" (Heb. 11:27). In the faith chapter of the Bible that means not the sense of sight, but faith. Unfortunately, however, that is not the kind of vision Joseph Smith claimed. But Mormons today need not perpetuate his error. On the basis of Scripture they can affirm their faith that God is invisible spirit.

Knowing that God is spirit, Mormons can then understand that the Bible employs many figures of speech from the material realm to designate that which is non-material. God's "eyes," "ears," "arms," and "face," are metaphorical terms referring to divine knowledge, strength, and presence. If it is foolish to think that God is a literal mother hen with wings and feathers (Ps. 91:4), it is equally foolish to think that God is a big physical man like Brigham Young. The image of God in man is not physical, but spiritual (Col. 3:10; Eph. 4:24).

Another Biblical figure of speech for God is "Father." Mormons attempt to take this literally, saying that God literally begets all the spirit-children in the pre-earth stage of existence. Jesus is the first of these literal sons, and hence is called the Son of God. In the Bible the phrase Son of God may be used of Jesus as conceived by the supernatural power of the Spirit (Lk. 1:35), but more frequently is parallel to the figures of "image," and "Word." These terms attempt to express in human language the eternal relationship between the first and second persons of the Trinity. The Second Person is eternally *of* the same divine nature as the Father, not physically, but spiritually. Mormons need help to see that they have become hyperliteralists to the point of contradicting Bible teaching that God is spirit, if not to the point of blasphemy against God Himself.

The doctrine of the Trinity provides an understanding of all the passages that Mormons use in support of a presiding council of separate Gods, and at the same time it incorporates all the passages which assert that God is one. Trinitarians believe, as do Mormons, that Father, Son, and Holy Spirit are three persons. But Trinitarians also believe, as the Bible and the Mormon scriptures teach, that God is one. "The Lord our God is one Lord" (Deut. 6:4). That is not merely a unity of mind or purpose, for as Paul said to the polytheists who called things gods in heaven and earth, ". . . there is none other God but one" (I Cor. 8:4). Only on the basis of Trinitarianism can we integrate Christ's and the Spirit's distinctness from the Father and Their oneness with the Father. Although denying their essential oneness, Lowell L. Bennion admits, "It is not always clear from the context of Scripture which of the three is meant, since their lives and missions are so intimately related."[55] Why not, then, fully affirm with the apostle John, "The Word was God" (Jn. 1:1)? Only those who receive Him have the authority to be called "children of God" (Jn. 1:12).

4. *Redemption*

As a Christian prayerfully attempts to direct a Latter-day Saint's attention to the gospel, he may ask another important question. "Do you believe Christ's shed blood is the only basis for the forgiveness of your sins?"

In answering this query Mormons will extol Christ's atonement. As Talmadge says:

> However incomplete may be our comprehension of the scheme of redemption through Christ's vicarious sacrifice in all its parts, we cannot reject it without becoming infidel; for it stands as the fundamental doctrine of all scripture, the very essence of the spirit of prophecy and revelation, the most prominent of all the declarations of God unto man.[56]

The *Book of Morman* is equally emphatic, "There could be no redemption for mankind save it were through the death and sufferings of Christ, and the atonement of his blood" (Alma 21:9).

Just why do the disciples of Joseph Smith think Christ's death so significant? It has accomplished marvelous things for the entire human race. "All men are thereby exonerated from the direct effects of the Fall (of Adam) in so far as such effects have been the cause of evil in their lives."[57] As a result of Adamic sin all men face physical death. But because of Christ's atonement all men will be raised from the dead. As a result of our first parents' sin all men are born with a natural inclination toward evil with its consequent guilt and condemnation. But because of Christ's death for them, all are "at one(ment)" with God again. Any infant or unaccountable person who dies "will be counted among the redeemed and sanctified."[58]

Wonderful as may be the universal benefits of Christ's atonement, it is of little avail for the normal living Mormon! Christ's death is not the basis of his forgiveness.

> We hold that salvation from sin is obtainable only through obedience, and that while the door to the kingdom has been opened by the sacrificial death and the resurrection of our Lord the Christ, no man may enter there except by his personal and voluntary application expressed in terms of obedience to the prescribed laws and ordinances of the Gospel.[59]

Christ's work only opens the door; man's work must do the rest. Christ makes the down payment; Mormons must make payments all of their lives.

For Mormons, then, the atonement was not completely provided by Christ. Elder Bruce R. McConkie ridicules the Christian belief that salvation is not on the ground of human merit, but of Christ's merit alone.

Christians speak often of the blood of Christ and its cleansing power. Much that is believed and taught on this subject, however, is such utter nonsense and so palpably false that to believe it is to lose ones salvation. Many go so far, for instance, as to pretend, at least, to believe that if we confess Christ with our lips and avow that we accept him as our personal Savior, we are thereby saved. His blood, without other act than mere belief, they say, makes us clean.[60]

Of course the doctrine of justification by faith on the merit of Christ's work alone can be distorted. But the faith that justifies is also the faith that works in love (Gal. 5:6). Whoever holds that the atoning work of Christ provided only an opportunity for people to achieve their own salvation has missed the heart of the Christian message.

Mormons, as desperately as others, need to hear of the good news of the justification by faith. It provides (1) pardon from all sin and (2) the perfect righteousness of Jesus Christ. A Mormon who accepts the teaching of his church fails to realize that keeping laws (even if called the laws of the gospel) never has been the basis of anyone's rightousness in the sight of God. The Scriptures declare, "By the deeds of the law there shall no flesh be justified in his sight: for by the law is the knowledge of sin" (Rom. 3:20). The righteousness the Bible teaches is "without," or apart from the law (Rom. 3:21). Believers are justified "freely by his grace through the redemption that is in Christ Jesus: Whom God hath set forth to be a propitiation through faith in his blood" (Rom. 3:24-25). Not just Christians, but the Scriptures teach that men are pardoned, God's law satisfied, and God's wrath propitiated, by acceptance of the completed atonement of Christ.

Mormon priests, like those of old, perform their works in vain. "And every priest standeth daily ministering and offering oftentimes the same sacrifices, which can never take away sins" (Heb. 10:11). How pitiful that Mormons still think salvation depends upon subservience to such priests, and that there can be no salvation outside their fold! They dare say, "Except men come to these legal administrators and learn of Christ and his laws as newly revealed on earth, they cannot be saved in his everlasting kingdom hereafter."[61] The works of Mormon priests are no more able to save than those of Israel's priests. What a contrast to the full assurance enjoyed by trusting Christ who by one sacrifice for sin "perfected forever them that are sanctified," (Heb. 10:14). Of believers, not law-keepers,

God says, "And their sins and iniquities will I remember no more" (10:17). Let every Mormon who would add his works to Christ's work remember Hebrews 10:18, "Now where remission of these is, there is no more offering for sin."

Tragically, Mormons do not realize that in addition to pardon from all their sin, they may have Christ's perfect righteousness ascribed to them. They have not known the joy David experienced— the blessedness of the man unto whom God imputeth righteousness without works (Rom. 4:6). Your Mormon friends have missed the happiness of Abraham who "believed God and it was counted unto him for righteousness" (Rom. 4:3,5,9,11,13,22). And why was so much written about Abraham's righteousness by faith? "Now it was not written for his sake alone, that it was imputed to him; but for us also, to whom it shall be imputed, if we believe on him that raised up Jesus our Lord from the dead" (Rom. 4:23-24).

Mormons who refuse the free gift of complete pardon and perfect righteousness are much like the Israelites of old. The apostle Paul said of them, ". . . they have a zeal of God, but not according to knowledge. For they, being ignorant of God's righteousness, and going about to establish their own righteousness, have not submitted themselves unto the righteousness of God" (Rom 10:2-3). And with Paul a twentieth century Christian says, "Brethren, my heart's desire and prayer to God for Israel (Latter-day Saints) is that they might be saved" (Rom. 10:1).

5. *The Resurrection of Christ*

A necessary condition of salvation, according to Romans 10:9-10, is belief that Jesus was raised from the dead. Do Mormons confess Christ's resurrection? They do. Talmadge well says:

> The facts of Christ's resurrection from the dead are attested by such an array of scriptural proofs that no doubt of the reality finds place in the mind of any believer in the inspired records.[62]

In support of this statement the usual texts are listed and supplemented with quotations from other Mormon "revelations." The great emphasis in Latter-day Saint writings falls on Christ's resurrection as the firstfruits of the resurrection of all men (Alma 33:22).

Grateful not to find an issue at this point, Christians will proceed more hopefully to the remaining questions.

6. *Personal Trust*

Faith involves intellectual assent to Christ's deity, death, and resurrection. But it involves more than that. The gospel's truths, like a long-awaited registered letter, bring to us something very valuable. By the Spirit of God they bring the living Christ to a sinner. The recipient of the registered letter personally signs that he has received its prized contents. Similarly individuals addressed by the gospel personally "sign" that they have received Christ by complete commitment to Him. Consequently a Christian concerned for a Mormon friend will ask, "Are you personally trusting Jesus Christ Himself as your redeemer and Lord?"

A Mormon who follows the teaching of his religion should have no hesitation in affirming that he has a vital commitment. For Mormonism, as for evangelical Christianity, faith is not mere belief, "merely intellectual assent," or "passive as an agreement or acceptance only." Rather, faith is active, positive, "vivified, vitalized, living belief."[63] It follows that "Faith in a passive sense, that is, as mere belief in the more superficial sense of the term, is inefficient as a means of salvation."[64] The faith that occasions exaltation is

> a principle of power . . . that impels men to resolve and act . . . Faith thus becomes to us the foundation of hope, from which spring our aspirations, ambitions, and confidences for the future. Remove man's faith in the possibility of any desired success, and you rob him of the incentive to strive.[65]

With this active view of faith, Christians heartily agree. But little seems to be written in Mormon literature about fellowship with the living Lord. Individual Mormons seem to be related to God only through the mediation of the institutional church and its sacraments. Since Latter-day Saints may not know the joy of personal communion with God through the one mediator, Jesus Christ (I Tim. 2:5), Christians may help significantly at this point by relating their own experience of fellowship with Christ. Add as well the witness of a mature Mormon who for two years studied the Bible while preparing to teach theology in an L.D.S. Relief Society. Carolyn J. Sexauer, in "My Testimony of the Grace of God," writes:

I came out of Mormonism.

Since that wonderful day when I gave up trying to reconcile the teachings of Mormonism with the Word of God, as found in the Bible, and was "born again" of the Spirit, I have been happier than ever before in my life, and have known in full measure "the peace of God that passeth all understanding."

I live each day rejoicing. Every burden on my heart is gone. Every doubt and fear is gone.

For a long time I have had the desire to bear my testimony to others who are members of the religion into which I was born and in which I have lived most of my life until now.

Space will not permit my going into detail as to my own desperate struggles, my uncertainty and despair before arriving at the truth, but oh I want to make it as clear as these poor words of mine can possibly do, how glorious it is to know the Lord Jesus Christ as my personal Saviour; to be absolutely certain of my salvation apart from anything I have done, or can do; to be a possessor of the indwelling Spirit of Christ — to live under the matchless grace of God.

It is the difference between the darkest night and the brightest day. Having found the Light, no power on earth could cause me to go back into darkness.[66]

In view of testimonies like this, a Mormon who claims to have a vital faith in Christ may not in fact have experienced redemption. He may be trusting not only in Christ, but also in his own works. He may be helped to see this by our last question.

7. *Faith Alone*

"Do you depend upon some achievements of your own for justification or do you rest upon God's grace received through faith alone?" Here a Mormon will take clear exception. He may even call the doctrine of justification by faith a pernicious error.

One wonders if the Mormon attack on the doctrine of justification by faith alone is based on understanding of it. The caricature of the doctrine ridiculed by Talmadge is not taught by the Christian church. As the writer of the standard doctrinal text of Mormonism puts it, "justification by *belief* alone" is "a most pernicious doctrine."[67] Indeed it is. But Christianity has never promulgated a dogma to the effect that "a wordy profession of belief shall open the doors of heaven to the sinner."[68] The atonement of Christ alone opens the doors of heaven. A sinner who by faith identifies himself with Christ is justified, not by what he has done, but by Christ's death. Saved by grace alone, works will follow, as James teaches. But works are not the basis on which God pardons sin and imputes righteousness. This doctrine has yet to be fairly stated and refuted in the Mormon literature.

How then do the Mormons find it possible to say they believe in grace alone? Bruce R. McConkie explains, "All men are *saved by grace alone* without any act on their part, meaning that they are resurrected and become immortal because of the atoning sacrifice of Christ."[69] Although you may be resurrected to judgment, your resurrection is by grace alone! You may be in torment, but your immortality is by grace alone! In addition, "all men by the grace of God have the power to gain eternal life. This is called *salvation by grace coupled with obedience* to the laws and ordinances of the gospel."[70] Then after ridiculing the idea of Christ's shed blood as the sole ground of forgiveness, the same writer adds, "Salvation in the kingdom of God is available because of the atoning blood of Christ. But it is received only on condition of faith, repentance, baptism, and enduring to the end in keeping the commandments of God."[71]

By adding works to faith, Mormons destroy the very essence of grace. According to Romans 11:6 God's election of his people is of grace, "And if by grace, then it is no more of works: otherwise grace is no more grace. But if it be of works, then it is no more grace: otherwise work is no more work." These principles are mutually exclusive because works receive a merited reward but grace is poured out upon those who are undeserving. Grace is unmerited favor, the free gift of God. The Mormon's attempted combination of works and faith reveals a misunderstanding of both. More than that, it destroys the good news. Mormons cannot sing,

> Jesus paid it all,
> All to Him I owe;
> Sin had left a crimson stain,
> *He* washed it white as snow.

Instead, Mormons write, "Does God help those who seek him? Yes, but all blessings are predicated upon obedience to law."[72] Propitiation from individual sins comes "through the faith and good works of the sinner," or "is conditioned on individual effort."[73] The phrase found so frequently in Mormon works, "the laws of the gospel," is *never* found in the Bible. As the books of Romans and Galatians state so emphatically, there can be no mixing of law and gospel or works and grace as the ground of justification before God.

In spite of Romans and Galatians, Mormon literature abounds with references to the four basic laws or principles of the gospel. These are usually listed as: (1) faith, (2) repentance, (3) baptism, and (4) laying on of hands by the Mormon priesthood for receiving the Holy Spirit. In view of such Scripture as Ephesians 2:8-10; Rom. 11:6; Gal. 2:16; it seems inconsistent to speak of faith and repentance as works. Together, repentant-faith, is the one act of turning to God from idols (I Thess. 1:9). As such repentant faith is not an achievement of man, but a forsaking of every humanly manufactured god and a complete casting of oneself upon Christ for His righteousness. Whoever depends upon his own works for justification has not begun to understand Biblical repentance or faith. They are the antithesis of human works! How then can they be classed as the first two works necessary to obey the laws of the gospel? The sinner who repents and trusts Christ is like the poor swimmer who finally realizes that left to his own efforts he would drown, ceases to struggle against the lifeguard, and completely relaxes in his care. Whoever claims that faith is just the beginning of salvation and that you must struggle to keep afloat the rest of your life has not faith.

The third and fourth principles of the Mormon gospel, baptism and the laying on of hands, also are believed necessary to justification. "Without these ordinances they could not be saved, says the scripture."[74] Mormons teach baptismal regeneration. "As a result of this act of obedience remission of sins is granted."[75] On the authority of *The Doctrines and Covenants* they hold one who is not baptized cannot be saved. The passage reads, "And he that believeth and is baptized shall be saved, and he that believeth not, and *is not baptized, shall be damned*" (112:29). Mark 16:16 does not add the last negative which is logically very strong. It is one thing to say, "He that is of age votes," but quite another to say, "Anyone who does not vote is not of age." (There could be other reasons for not voting.) It is one thing to say as Mark 16:16 does, "He that believeth and is baptized shall be saved," and quite another to say, as Joseph Smith does, "He that believeth not and *is not baptized* shall be damned." Baptism becomes essential for Mormons because they think it is "the means whereby each sinner may receive a cleansing from his past."[76]

It is not merely baptism that is necessary to pardon from sin, but baptism by the Mormon officials! "Remission of sins comes to the repentant believer through baptism, when it is performed by divine direction and under divine authority."[77] A L.S.D. tract entitled, "Baptism, How and By Whom Administered?" pontificates, "In order for the ordinance to be effectual, it must be performed by one authorized to act in the name of the Lord."[78] That means, called as was Aaron "by the voice of God." Now only Joseph Smith and the Mormon officials meet this test. And the same source insists, Christ "does not acknowledge unauthorized actions." Since baptism by Mormon officials is essential to salvation, it is not difficult to understand why the living are baptized vicariously for the dead. Millions died without this ordinance before the time of Joseph Smith, and since his day. People now can be baptized for their relatives. Consequently Mormons pursue "endless genealogies" and think they help many people to salvation by repeated baptisms.

Needless to say, the Bible in its extensive passages on justification (Rom. 3:21 - 5:21; Gal. 2 - 3), does not teach that baptism is a ground of justification. Passages in the Gospels and Acts must be interpreted, then, as intending that repentant-faith is the sole condition of justification, while baptism in water is the immediate outward expression of faith. Normally, every Christian is baptized, but baptism is not that which washes away his sin. A person is justified by faith, not by baptism. Baptism is a work; works are not the basis of imputed righteousness. Baptism is the first act of obedience to the Master whom the believer trusts and loves. And nowhere in the Bible is baptism to be performed by Aaronic priests. The priesthood is done away by the perfect work of Christ (Heb. 5 and 7). Now every believer is a priest of God (I Pet. 2:5,9). Baptism on behalf of the dead is nowhere *taught* in Scripture, although there is an allusion to a practice of baptism for the dead which Mormons often quote (I Cor. 15:29). Whatever its purpose (which may have been very different from that of present-day Mormonism), the practice is not commanded anywhere in Scripture. Surely if souls would be condemned apart from proxy baptism an extensive passage of Scripture would clearly teach this. In fact it should appear in the great commission! Sound Bible interpreters do not base any major doctrine upon one such incidental, ambiguous mention.

There remains the fourth work of laying on hands. Talmadge explains that all the ministries of the Holy Spirit are dependent upon this ceremony.

> The bestowal of the Holy Ghost, which is to be regarded as a conferred right to His ministrations, is effected through the ordinance of the Holy Priesthood, accompanied by the imposition of the hands of him or those officiating.[79]

Scripturally, the Holy Spirit comes upon all who believe (Rom. 8:9, 14; I Cor. 12:13). The apostles in some cases laid hands upon groups previously unassociated with the Jews or unaware of Christ's coming, but these instances in no way prove that after the time of the apostolic eyewitnesses of the risen Christ, this practice should be required of everyone. In all the epistles with their extensive teaching on the work of the Holy Spirit, nothing makes it dependent upon any such human ceremony.

Mormons who think a particular observance of baptism and laying on of hands necessary to salvation, desperately need to be confronted with passages like Galatians 2:16. What did Paul write to these who mixed works and faith in his day?

> Knowing that a man is not justified by the works of the law, but by the faith of Jesus Christ, even we have believed in Jesus Christ, that we might be justified by the faith of Christ, and not by the works of the law: for by the works the law shall no flesh be justified.

As much as any member of legalistic non-Christian religions, Mormons need to learn the truth of Ephesians 2:8-10:

> For by grace are ye saved through faith; and that not of yourselves: it is the gift of God: Not of works, lest any man should boast. For we are his workmanship, created in Christ Jesus unto good works, which God hath before ordained that we should walk in them.

Surely works will follow genuine faith. We are reminded many times by the Mormons that James said, "Faith without works is dead," and Jesus said, "If ye love me, keep my commandments." But what Mormons fail to see is that we are brought into the family of God by acceptance of the Son of God. As regenerated children of God we then behave like sons. That behavior is not the reason we are sons, but the result of sonship (Jn. 1:12-13). Or, as adopted children we behave like sons. But conduct as members of the family does not obtain sonship for us; it demonstrates sonship. If a regenerated and legally adopted son of God should disobey his divine parent — as all do — he does not lose his sonship. He loses fellowship, and the loving Father chastens his sons (Heb. 12:5-11). Christ then becomes the erring child's advocate with the Father (I Jn. 2:1). Parents know that no child can live up to the standards of perfection; they do not disown children for failing to keep every rule. If divine sonship depended on keeping the law there would be no sons! No one ever was saved by keeping the law (Rom. 3:10-23). But children of God by faith lovingly seek to do their divine Father's will. Mormons may say people will then sin that grace may abound (Rom. 6:1). The fact that they raise the same objection to Christian doctrine that was raised against Paul's teaching, is good evidence Christians have the Scriptural view.

Dr. Harry Ironside, once called on by a Mormon missionary, asked, "And now, sir, would you kindly favor us with a short statement of what the gospel really is?"

"Certainly," he replied. "The gospel consists of four first principles. The first is faith; the second, repentance; the third, baptism for the remission of sins by one duly qualified; while the fourth is the laying on of hands of a man having authority, for the reception of the Holy Ghost."

Dr. Ironside then said, "Well, supposing one has gone through all this, is he then saved?"

The Mormon replied, "Oh, of course, no one can know that, in this life. If one goes on to the end, he will be exalted in the kingdom."[80]

That is a clear example of Wesley P. Walter's judgment:

> Mormonism completely misses real salvation *and exaltation* as a free gift of God's grace. The Gospel is reduced to laws and ordinances brought to men by a Christ whose only function as Savior is to guaran-

tee to men a resurrection. To those enmeshed in a religion so materialistic in emphasis and so lacking in reverence, evangelical Christianity must hold out an all-sufficient Savior who saves, sanctifies, *and glorifies* unworthy sinners who place all their confidence in Him alone.[81]

As a result of just such an approach Albert Place, for 29 years a Mormon, found Christ. An earnest Latter-day Saint, he sought to convert others in the army. But Monty Burgeson puzzled him. Monty listened while Albert Place read the *Book of Mormon*, and then quietly said, "But what about Jesus Christ and His salvation?" After attending Monty's church Place gradually began to understand what his friend meant. Let Albert Place give his own witness: "At a Bible conference in the church the speaker taught from the books of Romans and Galatians. For the first time in my life, I realized that salvation comes through faith in Christ's perfect work, not in my own works, regardless of how good. Further Bible study led me personally to make Christ my Savior and Lord."[82] Within a year Place had led his father, mother, brother, and sister to Christ. Now he serves the Lord as a missionary to Mormons in Salt Lake City, Utah. May other missionaries of Joseph Smith become missionaries of Jesus Christ as Christians confront them with the gospel of God's grace!

FOOTNOTES

1. Edwin Scott Gaustad, *Historical Atlas of Religion in America* (New York: Harper & Row, Publishers, 1962), p. 87.
2. *The World Almanac and Book of Facts for 1965*, p. 706.
3. Personal letter of Horace A. Christiansen, President of the Western States Mission, to Gordon Lewis, May 30, 1963.
4. Gordon B. Hinckley, *What of the Mormons?* (Salt Lake City, Utah: The Church of Jesus Christ of Latter-day Saints, 1947), pp. 17-19.
5. *Ibid.,* p. 19.   6. *Ibid.,* p. 30.   7. *Ibid.*
8. "Mormon Dynamo," *Time*, May 20, 1957, p. 48.
9. *The Denver Post*, Dec. 27, 1958, p. 5.
10. Robert W. Fenwick, "Saints on the March," *The Denver Post*, April 7, p. 60.
11. Hartzell Spence, "The Mormons," *Look*, Jan. 21, 1958, p. 57.
12. Horace A. Christiansen, *op. cit.*
13. *A Brief Statement of the Principles of the Gospel* (Salt Lake City: Church of Jesus Christ of Latter-day Saints, 1943), p. 222.
14. James E. Talmadge, *Articles of Faith* (Salt Lake City, Utah: Church of Jesus Christ of Latter-day Saints, 1952), p. 466.
15. *Ibid.,* p. 504.
16. "Statement Regarding the Book of Mormon," Smithsonian Institution, Bureau of American Ethnology, Washington 25, D. C., July 22, 1960.
17. Joseph Smith, *The Pearl of Great Price* (Salt Lake City, Utah: George Q. Cannon and Sons, 1891), pp. 68-69.
18. *Ibid.*
19. Walter R. Martin, *The Maze of Mormonism* (Grand Rapids, Michigan: Zondervan Publishing House, 1962), pp. 42-44 (Reprints the entire letter of Charles Anthon.)
20. Cited by Arthur Budvarson, *The Book of Mormon Examined* (LaMesa, California: The Utah Christian Tract Society, 1959), p. 11.
21. *Ibid.*   22. *Ibid.*
23. John L. Smith, *Has Mormonism Changed?* (Clearfield, Utah: The Utah Evangel Press, 1961), p. 34.
24. Arthur Budvarsson, *op. cit.,* p. 22.
25. Walter R. Martin, *op. cit.,* pp. 51-53.
26. The testimony of the three and eight witnesses is quoted in the introductory pages of the *Book of Mormon.*
27. Cited by G. T. Harrison, *Mormons Are a Peculiar People* (New York: Vantage Press, 1954), p. 91.
28. *Ibid.,* pp. 90-91.
29. James E. Talmadge affirms of only three of the witnesses that they died "in full fellowship" with the church, *op. cit.,* p. 503. All of the three witnesses apostacized, Martin, *op. cit.,* p. 51; and five of the eight witnesses defected from the Church, Budvarson, *op. cit.,* pp. 22, 26.

30. J. H. Beadle, *Life in Utah* (Philadelphia: National Publishing Co., 1870), p. 32.

31. G. T. Harrison, *op. cit.*, pp.12-20; Larry Jonas, *Mormon Claims Examined* (Grand Rapids: Baker Book House, 1961), pp. 30-39, 44.

32. Larry Jonas, *op. cit.*, pp. 21,26.

33. Walter R. Martin, *op. cit.*, pp. 22-25.

34. "Compass," *World Book Encyclopedia*, III, 735.

35. "French Language," *World Book Encyclopedia*, VI, 443.

36. Walter R. Martin, *op. cit.*, p. 53.

37. "Jackson, Andrew," *World Book Encyclopedia*, X, 11.

38. G. T. Harrison, *op. cit.*, p. 167.

39. Cited by Hal Houghey, *Archeology and the Book of Mormon* (Concord, California: Pacific Publishing Co., n.d.), pp. 5-6.

40. *Ibid.*   41. *Ibid.*

42. John L. Smith, *op. cit.*, p. 9.

43. Vergilius Ferm, ed., *Religion in the Twentieth Century* (New York: The Philosophical Library, 1948), pp. 289-305.

44. Leo Rosten, ed., *A Guide to the Religions of America* (New York: Simon and Schuster, 1955), pp. 92-93.

45. Rulon S. Howells, *The Mormon Story* (Salt Lake City: Bookcraft, 1963), p. 30.

46. James E. Talmadge, *The Philosophical Basis of Mormonism* (Independence, Missouri: Zion's Printing and Publishing Co., 1915), p. 7.

47. Lowell L. Bennion, *The Religion of the Latter-day Saints* (Salt Lake City: L.D.S. Department of Education, 1940), p. 57.

STAGES AND OPPORTUNITIES
IN MAN'S ETERNAL LIFE

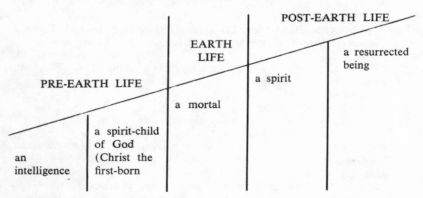

48. Bruce R. McConkie, *What the Mormons Think of Christ* (Salt Lake City: L.D.S. Missionary Committee, n.d.), p. 31.

49. Wallace F. Bennett, *Why I Am a Mormon* (New York: Thomas Nelson and Sons, 1958), p. 216.
50. James E. Talmadge, *op. cit.*, p. 13.
51. James E. Talmadge, *Articles of Faith*, p. 39.
52. *Ibid.*, p. 40.   53. *Ibid.*, p. 43.   54. *Ibid.*, p. 42.
55. Lowell L. Bennion, *op. cit.*, p. 32.
56. James E. Talmadge, *Articles of Faith*, p. 77.
57. James E. Talmadge, *The Philosophical Basis of Mormonism*, p. 15.
58. *Ibid.*, p. 16.   59. *Ibid.*, p. 17.
60. Bruce R. McConkie, *op. cit.*, p. 27.
61. *Ibid.*, p. 7
62. James E. Talmadge, *Articles of Faith*, pp. 385-386.
63. *Ibid.*, pp. 96-97.   64. *Ibid.*, p. 107.   65. *Ibid.*, pp. 102-103.
66. Carolyn J. Sexauer, *My Testimony of the Grace of God* (Helmet, Calif.: Christian Tract Society, n.d.), pp. 3-4.
67. James E. Talmadge, *op. cit.*, p. 107.
68. *Ibid.*, p. 108.
69. Bruce R. McConkie, *op. cit.*, p. 24.
70. *Ibid.*   71. *Ibid.*, p. 28.
72. Gordon B. Hinckley, *op. cit.*, p. 23.
73. James E. Talmadge, *op. cit.*, pp. 87, 89.
74. Samuel O. Bennion, *Fundamental Principles of the Gospel* (Salt Lake City: L.D.S. Missionary Department, n.d.), p. 35.
75. James E. Talmadge, *Articles of Faith*, p. 120.
76. Charles W. Penrose, *Repentance and Baptism* (Salt Lake City: Church of Jesus Christ of Latter-day Saints, n.d.), p. 5.
77. *Ibid.*
78. *Baptism, How, and By Whom Administered?* (Salt Lake City: Deseret News Press, n.d.), p. 2-3.
79. James E. Talmadge, *Articles of Faith*, p. 165.
80. H. A. Ironside, "The Mormon's Mistake," *Religious Research Digest* I (October - December, 1961), pp. 12-13.
81. Wesley P. Walters, "Mormonism," *Christianity Today*, December 19, 1960, p. 10 (230).
82. Albert Place, "I Was a Mormon," *Power*, May 8, 1955, p. 3.

FOR FURTHER STUDY

ARTHUR BUDVARSON, *The Book of Mormon Examined* (La Mesa, Calif.: The Utah Christian Tract Society, 1959). A 47 page booklet with photographic reproductions from the Book of Mormon.

LARRY W. JONAS, *Mormon Claims Examined* (Grand Rapids, Michigan: Baker Book House, 1961). An 85-page booklet with documented evidence answering Mormon claims.

WALTER R. MARTIN, *The Maze of Mormonism* (Grand Rapids, Michigan: Zondervan Publishing House, 1962). A thorough discussion and evangelical apraisal of Mormonism's history and teaching.

JOHN L. SMITH, *Has Mormonism Changed?* (Clearfield, Utah: Utah Evangel Press, 1961). In 62 pages a Southern Baptist preacher who has served many years in Utah shares his experience in witnessing to Mormons. He also publishes: *Hope or Despair?* (35 pp.), *Thirty-five Mormons and One Baptist Preacher* (48 pp.), and *120 Questions to ask Mormon Missionaries.*

SUGGESTIONS FOR TEACHERS

Good Teaching is marked by clarity of purpose. Review the content of this study and attempt to synthesize it in your own mind. This material may best be divided into two sections for two teaching sessions. Put into a few words a statement of objectives for classroom presentation. *Confronting the Cults* differs from some other works on the subject in that its purpose is not primarily negative — refuting false doctrine, but positive — winning cultists to to Christ.

1. Use the lead questions throughout the series to form the major divisions of the teaching sessions. Illustrate the way these questions keep discussion centered on the gospel by moving back to them from irrelevant issues.
2. Anticipate replies Christians may expect to these questions from Latter-day Saints. Evaluate the Mormon position and give specific guidance in answering erroneous beliefs.
3. Build confidence for effective personal witness by helping your group formulate possible approaches and answers. Use simple role playing situations to involve the group in learning the major doctrines of Mormonism. After the material has been studied allow several people to take the position of the cultist in confronting the believer. Let others assume the role of a believer. Simulate a conversation. Try various ways of presenting the truth in the face of error.
4. Secure a copy of the *Book of Mormon* (and possibly also *Doctrines and Covenants* and *Pearl of Great Price*) published by the Church of Jesus Christ of Latter-day Saints, Salt Lake City, Utah. Interested class members also may wish a copy to mark for use in witnessing to members of this cult. Passages revealing contradictions and historical discrepancies could be marked in one way, and verses for leading Mormons to Christ in another way.
5. Ask members of the class to give their personal testimony of salvation by grace apart from works as they would to missionaries of the Mormon church. Especially urge those who depended on a system of works prior to salvation to participate in this.

Latter-day Saints

SAMPLE LESSON PLAN

SESSION 1

Aim

To guide the class to a knowledge of Mormon teaching on divine authority.
To help the class develop skills of witnessing to those who accept books
other than the Bible as divine revelation.

Approach

Lead a discussion on reasons for the phenomenal growth of Mormonism.
What can Christians learn about propagating the faith from Mormons?

Outline

Divine Authority, revelation, inspiration
Question: "Do you base your teachings on revelations other than the
Bible?"

A. On a blackboard list inconsistencies in the Mormon revelations.
B. List ways in which these revelations fail to fit facts.
C. List tests of a true prophet and give Joseph Smith a grade of passing
or failing.

Conclusion

Sum up answers to Mormon claims of revelation from God in addition to
the Bible. Discuss ways of presenting this material to Mormons. Would
it best to start with criticisms of Mormon revelations, or another subject?

SESSION 2

Aim

To guide the class to a knowledge of Mormon teaching about the gospel,
Christ, redemption, Christ's resurrection, and personal faith.
To help the class members develop skill in handling the Scriptures as they
witness to Mormons.

Approach

Review briefly the previous lesson and set an attitude favorable to helping
cultists, not embarrassing them.

41

Outline

I. The Gospel
   Question: "Is your main business the proclamation of the gospel of Jesus Christ?"

II. The Doctrine of Christ
   Question: "Do you believe that Jesus is the Christ, the eternal Word of God who has come in the flesh?"

III. Redemption
   Question: "Do you believe that Jesus died for your sins?"

IV. The Resurrection of Jesus Christ
   Question: "Do you believe that Jesus Christ arose from the dead bodily?"

V. Personal Faith
   Question: "Are you personally trusting Jesus Christ as your Redeemer and Lord?"
   Question: "Do you depend upon some achievements of your own to contribute to your justification, or is it only by way of God's grace through faith?"

Conclusion

Sum up the Scriptural teaching on these subjects and challenge the class to be as zealous in witnessing to Mormons as Mormons are in seeking to reach them!